WHEN HARRIET MET SOJOURNER

By CATHERINE CLINTON · Illustrated by SHANE W. EVANS

KATHERINE TEGEN BOOKS

An Imprint of HarperCollinsPublishers

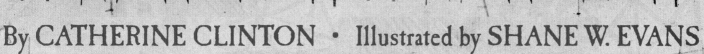

Dedicated to Julie & Carla Anne and Deborah & Jody,
because we make new friends but keep the old—and you are my silver and my gold.

—C.C.

Thank you, God. Dedicated to my daughter, Yurie.

—S.W.E.

Photo of Sojourner Truth courtesy of the Library of Congress, LC-USZ62-119343
Photo of Harriet Tubman courtesy of the Library of Congress, LC-USZ62-7816

Amistad is an imprint of HarperCollins Publishers.

Library of Congress Cataloging-in-Publication Data
Clinton, Catherine, 1952–
    When Harriet met Sojourner / by Catherine Clinton ; illustrated by Shane W. Evans. — 1st ed.
        p.   cm.
    ISBN-10: 0-06-050425-0 (trade bdg.) — ISBN-13: 978-0-06-050425-0 (trade bdg.)
    ISBN-10: 0-06-050426-9 (lib. bdg.) — ISBN-13: 978-0-06-050426-7 (lib. bdg.)
    1. Tubman, Harriet, 1820?–1913—Juvenile literature. 2. Truth, Sojourner, d. 1883—Juvenile literature. 3. African Americans—Biography—
Juvenile literature. 4. African American women—Biography—Juvenile literature. 5. Slaves—United States—Biography—Juvenile literature. 6. African
American abolitionists—Biography—Juvenile literature. 7. Social reformers—United States—Biography—Juvenile literature. 8. Boston (Mass.)—
History—Civil War, 1861–1865—Juvenile literature. I. Evans, Shane, ill. II. Title.
E444.T82C58 2007   2006019099
973.7'1150922—dc22
[B]

Typography by Sarah Hoy
❖
1 2 3 4 5 6 7 8 9 10

First Edition

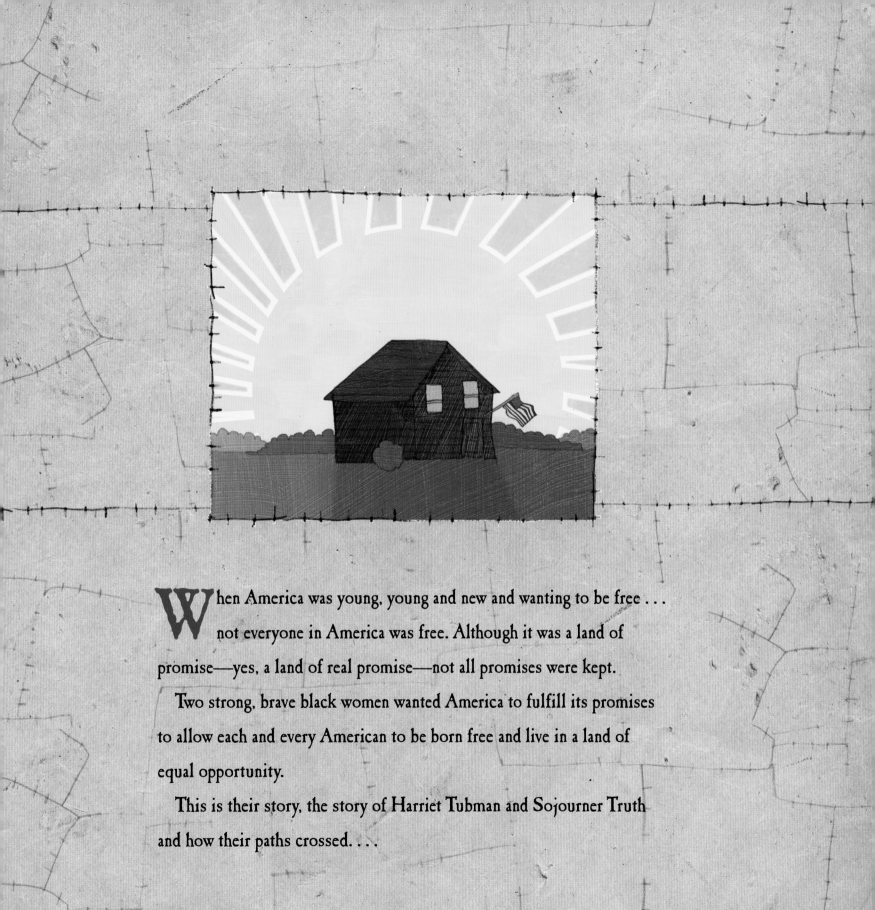

When America was young, young and new and wanting to be free . . .
not everyone in America was free. Although it was a land of
promise—yes, a land of real promise—not all promises were kept.

Two strong, brave black women wanted America to fulfill its promises
to allow each and every American to be born free and live in a land of
equal opportunity.

This is their story, the story of Harriet Tubman and Sojourner Truth
and how their paths crossed. . . .

Sojourner Truth was born first—some day, sometime around 1797, near the Hudson Valley, in upstate New York. She was born the daughter of enslaved parents, parents owned by a wealthy Dutch planter. They gave her the name Isabella, and she took her father's name, Bomefree.

Isabella Bomefree—Bomefree, but not free.

Bomefree means "tall tree" in Dutch. The name suited Isabella well. She grew strong and tall, bending like a willow while working the fields alongside her twelve brothers and sisters.

As the crow flies hundreds of miles south from Isabella's birthplace, it might alight on the eastern shore of Maryland, where sometime around 1825 a young slave girl named Araminta was born.

Araminta's parents loved and cherished their sons and daughters but could not protect them from the evils of slavery.

Two of her sisters were snatched away, stolen off and sold South—they were gone but never forgotten.

Araminta dreamed of freedom, of flying away with her whole family. She did not know how or when but yearned for flight. One day, in freedom, she would be known as Harriet Tubman.

Isabella this and Isabella that! Forced to obey a parade of masters, from dawn to dusk. Sent from farm to farm, away from her brothers and sisters, away from her parents. Poor Isabella.

Once she was sent to a farm where they spoke only English. She spoke Dutch and could not understand, could not make herself understood.

She tried and tried to be good and obedient, and everyone knew she was a good worker. But an English master called her names—and even beat her.

She vowed when she grew up, she would leave slavery behind and be poor Isabella no more. She would defeat those who had tried to defeat her, and rename herself Sojourner Truth.

Araminta, too, worked hard, moving from one master to another, hired out from the age of seven. But one day when one of her friends from the fields was trying to get away from an angry overseer, Araminta tried to protect him. When the overseer threw a heavy piece of lead, it hit Araminta instead of her friend—smashing in her skull and knocking her to the ground. She was almost killed!

Carried home half-dead, Araminta was nursed by her mother, who sat by her daughter's bedside and told Bible stories— of David and Goliath, of Daniel in the lion's den, of Moses and the Red Sea. It was nearly a miracle when she finally recovered. But Harriet's scar would always be with her, a reminder of slavery's evils and a symbol of her courage and willingness to help others.

Isabella grew and grew until she was six feet tall. She was one of the strongest workers in the field, and not a man could best her! She worked hard, but a yearning for freedom rose like sap within her. She married another slave and had five children, her daughters and son like branches reaching from her sturdy trunk.

When New York passed a law outlawing slavery after 1827, Isabella thought that God had answered her prayers. Her master promised to free her in a year. She counted the months and weeks and days until she might leave slavery behind.

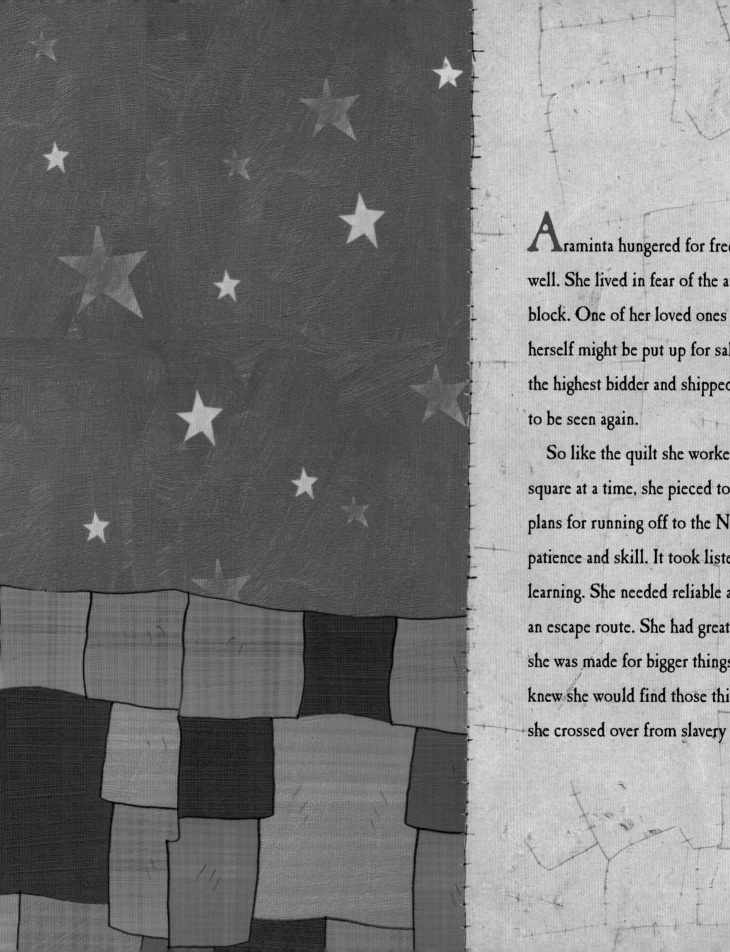

Araminta hungered for freedom as well. She lived in fear of the auction block. One of her loved ones or she herself might be put up for sale, sold to the highest bidder and shipped off, never to be seen again.

So like the quilt she worked on, one square at a time, she pieced together her plans for running off to the North. It took patience and skill. It took listening and learning. She needed reliable advice about an escape route. She had great faith, faith she was made for bigger things. And she knew she would find those things, once she crossed over from slavery to freedom.